T0001315

ideals®
CHRISTMAS

Bring lanterns, laughter to the streets;
bring promises and songs and sweets;
bring sleepy babes; bring broken hearts;
bring love in pockets, baskets, carts;
bring soup and books and dreams to share:
there's magic in December's air.

—EILEEN SPINELLI

ideals®

NASHVILLE, TENNESSEE

Winter Jewels
Renee A. Gardner

Sun on the snow, a radiant sight,
moon on the snow, jewels by night;
snow gently falling from darkened skies,
blanket the earth with a white paradise.

Against the sky, the blackened trees
are prisoned in their crystal sheaths;
when sun strikes their branches with heavenly light,
it creates a brilliant, most wondrous sight.

The rivers are frozen and so are the streams,
making glittering patterns of wintry scenes;
designs that dazzle the human eye,
created for us by Him on high.

The jewels of man cannot compare
with the beauties of nature, so lovely, so rare;
mankind creates unlimited treasures,
yet one snowflake is unique beyond measure.

Snowflakes
Adlai A. Esteb

Beautiful snowflakes, so lovely and bright,
robing the earth with a mantle of white,
patterns of beauty delighting the eye
falling so gracefully out of the sky.

Each dainty flake has a gorgeous design,
carved in the clouds by a hand that's divine,
bearing a message of infinite worth,
lessons of love from heaven to earth.

Oh, that our love were as pure and as white
as beautiful snowflakes reflecting the light;
diamonds of glory, you soon will depart;
you've brought a treasure to my happy heart.

Image © Leonid Ikan/Adobe Stock

Winter Dress
Maxine Bell

Have you ever gone a-walking
on a clear, cold winter night,
when the air was clear and frosty
and the snow lay mounded white?

Have you walked along a street,
seen houses gay and bright;
have you seen a grinning snowman
standing near the old streetlight?

Have you tramped in snow, knee-deep,
and seen sparkling diamonds gleam,

or walked along a snowy bank
of a still and frozen stream?

Have you seen the leafless branches
of trees bent low with snow
or stood in awestruck wonder
of northern lights aglow?

Have you seen a dainty snowflake
or icicles shimmering splintery?
Then you've seen the wondrous beauty
of a world all dressed for winter.

Winter Walk
Marguerite Gode

Big shoes and little shoes
walking in the snow
leave a trail of footprints
everywhere they go.
In and out the garden gate,
up and down the street,
there are snowy imprints
of their trudging feet.

Big shoes walk sedately,
small shoes skip and run,
sending clouds of snow dust
in their outdoor fun.
Here they spy a squirrel's nest
high up in a tree,
weaving patterns deep and white
as they stop to see.

By the feeding tray they turn
to see the winter brood
of starlings from the northland
come in search of food.
Bushes flaunt their powdered lace,
trees are traced in chalk,
it's a day for any shoes
to take a winter walk.

Image © Casey McCallister/Stocksy

Homecoming

Edgar A. Guest

I watch them at the depot,
the mothers at the gate,
who ask the age-old question:
"Is the train on time or late?"
The annual tears of gladness,
the same sweet laughter gay,
the loved ones home returning
to spend the Christmas Day.

I watch them staring, peering,
along the railroad track
and think how glad the season
that brings the loved ones back!

How long and bleak the absence
of those obliged to roam!
But, oh, the joy of Christmas
which brings the children home!

Oh, glorious, happy moment
when love flings wide the door!
The family united;
the table filled once more.
The mother and the father,
the grandfolks all content.
Oh, little Child of Bethlehem,
all this your coming meant.

The Heart Turns Home for Christmas

Linda C. Grazulis

The heart turns home for
    Christmas,
decked out in holly and mistletoe,
to laughter shared and carols sung
and hearth fires set aglow.

We might be snowbound for the day
and can't squeeze out the door;
but oh, the merriment inside:
sweet memories, shared joys,
    and more.

Chestnuts are roasting,
    popcorn strung,
the green tree shelters many a toy,
gingerbread men, peppermint canes,
and piles of cards to enjoy.

Home candles are flickering hope
    to mankind
as from the windows they portray
peace to the heart, an inner glow,
and faith to light the way.

HOMECOMING by John Sloane. Image © John Sloane

A Small-Town Christmas

Christine Phillips Blagden

I grew up in a small town in the 1960s; and at the first sign of snow in November, the town's utility workers scurried to transform the main shopping street—Thames Street—into a magical winter wonderland. Two enormous bells, made from freshly cut cedar boughs, were raised high above the traffic to adorn the two main intersections. As the first snowflakes settled on the bells, they created a delicate lace design on the deep green boughs.

Wreaths of cedar hung from the top of each lamppost that lighted the snow-covered sidewalks and brick and cobblestone streets. Folks took advantage of the snow and flocked to town in horse-drawn wagons and sleighs, and the clip-clop of the horses' hooves echoed in the distance as families snuggled under heavy blankets.

November waned and the shop windows on Thames Street came to life as toy trains chugged in circles, brightly colored tops spun round and round, wind-up jacks-in-the-box perpetually popped up and down, and marionettes never tired of performing for the shoppers. Children, wide-eyed with excitement and wonder, pressed their noses to the cold windowpanes to consider if their requests to Santa would include Raggedy Ann and Andy dolls to cuddle and hug, multicolored pick-up sticks to play with a friend, or Tinker Toys and Erector sets for building castles or skyscrapers or tractors.

At the end of Thames Street sat the bakery which greeted every customer with the smell of freshly baked shortbread, festive holiday breads, and cherry-topped Chelsea buns. Who could resist the allure of the peppery gingerbread cookies, shaped and frosted into bells, snowmen, wreaths, and, of course, gingerbread men and women? The last stop on the trip to town was the grocer's. More sugar for cookies and fudge, flour for pies, the Christmas turkey, potatoes, and most importantly, the ingredients for the pièce de résistance: the holiday plum pudding.

Now every year, as the days shorten and Christmas approaches, I experience a wistfulness, a yearning for the town of my childhood. Of course, the town still exists, but it is no longer the one of my youth. The small town of my childhood has changed, but my memories remain as warm and as tender as Christmas Day itself.

Image © Ju_see/Adobe Stock

Christmas Ornaments
Valerie Worth

The boxes break at the corners,
their sides sink weak;
they are tied up every year
with the same gray string;
but under the split lids, a fortune
shines: globes of gold and sapphire,
silver spires and bells, jeweled
nightingales with pearly tails.

O Christmas Tree
Author Unknown

O Christmas Tree, O Christmas tree,
how lovely are your branches!
O Christmas Tree, O Christmas tree,
how lovely are your branches!

Not only green in summer's heat,
but also winter's snow and sleet.
O Christmas tree, O Christmas tree,
how lovely are your branches!

O Christmas Tree, O Christmas tree,
of all the trees most lovely;
O Christmas Tree, O Christmas tree,
of all the trees most lovely.

Each year you bring to us delight
with brightly shining Christmas light!
O Christmas Tree, O Christmas tree,
of all the trees most lovely.

Image © Felix Mittermeier/Pixabay

Mistletoe

Walter de la Mare

Sitting under the mistletoe
(pale-green, fairy mistletoe),
one last candle burning low,
all the sleepy dancers gone,
just one candle burning on,
shadows lurking everywhere:
someone came, and kissed me there.

Tired I was; my head would go
nodding under the mistletoe
(pale-green, fairy mistletoe),
no footsteps came, no voice, but only,
just as I sat there, sleepy, lonely,
stooped in the still and shadowy air
lips unseen—and kissed me there.

The Christmas Holly

Eliza Cook

The holly! The holly!
    Oh, twine it with bay—
come give the holly a song;
for it helps to drive stern winter away,
with his garment so somber and long.
It peeps through the trees
    with its berries of red
and its leaves of burnish'd green,
when the flowers and fruits
    have long been dead,
and not even the daisy is seen.
Then sing to the holly,
    the Christmas holly,
that hangs over peasant and king;
while we laugh and carouse
    'neath its glitt'ring boughs,
to the Christmas holly we'll sing.

The gale may whistle,
    and frost may come,
to fetter the gurgling rill;
the woods may be bare,
    and the warblers dumb—
but the holly is beautiful still.
In the revel and light of princely halls,
the bright holly-branch is found;
and its shadow falls
    on the lowliest walls,
while the brimming horn goes round.
Then drink to the holly,
    the Christmas holly,
that hangs over peasant and king;
while we laugh and carouse
    'neath its glitt'ring boughs,
to the Christmas holly we'll sing.

Image © Juliette Wade/GAP Photos

Songs of the Season

Pamela Kennedy

In the Gospel account of the first Christmas, Luke describes a great heavenly host appearing to shepherds, praising God, and saying, "Glory to God in the highest heaven, and on earth peace to those on whom his favor rests" (Luke 2:14 NIV). According to some, this was the first Christmas carol. Scripture, however, doesn't say they actually sang these words. In fact, there wasn't much singing going on at Christmas for almost fifteen hundred years after the birth of Christ! And even then, the first Christmas carols weren't associated with the religious celebration of Christ's birth. They were, instead, modified drinking and dancing songs about secular winter festivals focused upon feasting and making merry with friends.

When, in 1647, the Puritan-led English parliament banned all Christmas celebrations, the singing of these carols along with other holiday festivities went underground. Eventually, with the lifting of the ban on Christmas in England in 1660, some of the earliest carols like "The Boar's Head Carol," "Good Christian Men Rejoice," and "The First Nowell" reappeared and, slowly, Christmas hymns and carols gained in popularity. It would take another 150 years before most of the carols we associate with Christmas were composed and set to music.

"Silent Night" was written in Austria by Catholic priest Joseph Mohr in 1816 and set to music by his friend Franz Gruber in 1818. It was first sung by the two men on Christmas Eve that year. Although "Hark the Herald Angels Sing" was penned as a poem by Charles Wesley in 1739, the melody wasn't composed by Felix Mendelssohn until almost 100 years later. The beloved carol "O Little Town of Bethlehem" was written by American Episcopal clergyman Phillip Brooks for the children in his Sunday school class in 1868. Shortly thereafter, his church organist, Lewis Redner, composed the melody; and it was first sung at that year's Christmas service in Philadelphia's Church of the Holy Trinity.

Interestingly, some of our favorite Christmas carols weren't really intended to be about Christmas at all! For example, "Jingle Bells" was written in the 1850s by James Lord Pierpont to describe the Thanksgiving sleigh races of his hometown in Massachusetts. "Deck the Halls" originated as a Welsh tune welcoming the New Year. "The Twelve Days of Christmas" originated in France as a children's game of "memory-and-forfeit" where the singer had to pay for any mistakes in recalling the correct order of items with candy or a kiss! "The Carol of the Bells" is a Ukrainian folk song celebrating the promise of a bountiful spring. Even "Joy to the World," one of the most beloved Christmas carols, wasn't originally written to celebrate Christmas. The text comes from a poetic interpretation of Psalm 98 by British hymn writer Isaac Watts and celebrates the second coming of Christ. The connection with Christmas didn't come until 1836 when American composer Lowell Mason, inspired by Handel's *Messiah*, set Watts's verses to music.

In the secular music world, with the invention of record players, radios, and eventually movies and television, Christmas music became more popular—and profitable. Songwriters vied to compose tunes that would find a place in the lexicon of holiday favorites. The mid-twentieth century was a particularly fruitful time for such songs. In 1942, when Bing Crosby and Marjorie Reynolds sang Irving Berlin's "White Christmas" in the movie *Holiday Inn*, they probably had no idea it would become a Christmas classic. Judy Garland, in the 1944 movie

Meet Me in St. Louis, gave us another holiday favorite as she sat in a window wistfully singing "Have Yourself a Merry Little Christmas." Although written decades ago, these Christmas favorites are still popular each holiday season.

Today, it's hard to imagine Christmas without music. Even though it wasn't always so, there seems no better way to communicate the joy and wonder of the season than with carols and songs, both religious and secular. From the majestic chords of "Joy to the World" to the nostalgia of "White Christmas," our journey through the holiday season wouldn't be nearly as delightful without the songs of the season.

Image © Africa Studio/Adobe Stock

Here We Come
A-Caroling

Author Unknown

Here we come a-caroling among the
    leaves so green;
Here we come a-wand'ring so fair
    to be seen.
Love and joy come to you,
and to you glad Christmas too,
and God bless you and send
you a happy new year,
and God send you a happy new year.

We are not daily beggars that beg
    from door to door,
but we are neighbors' children
    whom you have seen before.
Love and joy come to you,
and to you glad Christmas too,
and God bless you and send
you a happy new year,
and God send you a happy new year.

God bless the master of this house,
    likewise the mistress too,
and all the little children that
    round the table go.
Love and joy come to you,
and to you glad Christmas too,
and God bless you and send
you a happy new year,
and God send you a happy new year.

Carol of the Bells

Author Unknown

Hark how the bells, sweet silver bells,
all seem to say, throw cares away,
Christmas is here, bringing good cheer,
to young and old, the meek and bold.

Ding dong, ding dong, that is their song
with joyful ring all caroling.
One seems to hear words of good cheer
from everywhere filling the air.

Oh, how they pound, raising the sound,
o'er hill and dale, telling their tale.
Gaily they ring while people sing
songs of good cheer, Christmas is here.

Merry, merry, merry, merry Christmas,
Merry, merry, merry, merry Christmas.
On, on they send, on without end,
their joyful tone to every home.
Ding dong, ding . . . dong!

Image © Daniel Rodgers/Advocate Art

Bits & Pieces

I wish we could put up some of the Christmas spirit in jars and open a jar of it every month.
—Harlan Miller

*N*ow that the time has come wherein our Saviour Christ was born, the larder's full of beef and pork, the granary's full of corn.
—Author Unknown

*F*or the spirit of Christmas fulfills the greatest hunger of mankind.
—Loring A. Schuler

*I*t won't be long till soon we taste baked turkey and stuffed goose, chestnuts and plum puddings, and cidered apple juice.
—Nellie Wailes Stokes

*C*hristmas tastes like crisp
apples and sweet tangerines,
pumpkin pie and fruitcake,
eggnog and cracked nuts, like
date cookies and hot chocolate.
—*Diana Smith Walls*

*C*ookies are an integral part of
Christmas. The house takes on the
excitement of the season as soon as the
first batch of cookies is baked and the
delicious aroma permeates the house.
—*Lela Bernard*

*C*hristmas is come, hang on the pot,
let spits turn round and ovens be hot;
beef, pork, and poultry now provide to
feast thy neighbors at this tide.
—*Virginia Almanack*

"A Merry Christmas to us all, my dears. God bless us!"
Which all the family re-echoed. "God bless us every one!"
said Tiny Tim, the last of all.
—*Charles Dickens*

Christmas Baking

Louise Weibert Sutton

Smiling, she rolled her dough with care,
cutting the cookies one by one,
some into stars and some to spare,
shaping like Santas, just for fun.
Cinnamon, raisin, butter, spice,
came from the oven warmly, sweetly.
What other smells could be so nice?
What other things so good to eat?

Filled to the brim, each cookie jar
waited for Santa's yearly whim;
"Santa knows where the cookies are,
and leave some coffee just for him!"
Maybe he'd like a midnight treat,
a chance to rock and doze a bit,
then when he's had enough to eat
he'll start again on his happy trip.

Here, and perhaps in other lands,
memory holds such cookie jars:
mothers who rolled, with careful hands,
spicy brown dough for Christmas stars,
raisin-fat Santas, ginger trees,
coconut angels to surprise
happy Saint Nick, or just to please
children who watched with shining eyes.

Image © New Africa/Adobe Stock

Dickens of a Christmas

Susan Sundwall

As I wound my way up and down the aisles of our local grocery store, my mind leaped to several scenes from Charles Dickens's *A Christmas Carol*. For once I was not in a particular hurry, frantically ticking off the items on my list, my mind set on what I had to do once I got home, and a hundred other things. I had time to be lost in the moment and reflect on the riches surrounding me.

How quickly the Ghost of Christmas Present, resplendent in his green robe trimmed with white fur, popped into my head. In every play or movie I've ever seen of this classic Christmas tale, this ghost is the most impressive. Inordinately tall, torch held on high, he sweeps his hand over the scene. At his feet lies a bounty that Charles Dickens explores in great detail. "Heaped up on the floor to form a kind of throne, were turkeys, geese, game, poultry, brawn, great joints of meat, suckling pigs, long wreaths of sausages, mince pies, plum puddings, barrels of oysters, red hot chestnuts, cherry cheeked apples, juicy oranges, luscious pears, immense twelfth cakes, seething bowls of punch that made their chamber dim with their delicious steam."

While our small local grocery store does a fair job of it, I'll have to admit it falls a bit short of Dickens's Horn of Plenty description by not stocking immense twelfth cakes or suckling pigs. Still, they do a great job of bringing the season forward for us otherwise. It starts just a wee wink before Thanksgiving and spreads across the country. I smile at the workers in produce and meats and applaud this insistence of merchants who join in with the celebratory practices of the people they serve. I'm amazed that so many of the directors in various grocery store corporate offices have read *A Christmas Carol* and seek to imitate the glorious bounty described therein.

I made a concerted effort to linger in the fruit and produce aisle, sucking up the citrus smells of the oranges and lemons, the earthy aromas of the potatoes and cabbages. I marveled at the loads of cheeses and spiced meats and jaunty Santa Claus hats on the scales at the deli counter. I was sorely tempted to ask about that suckling pig. In the drinks aisle the red and green bottles of Coca-Cola and Sprite seemed to greet me as I strolled past. The end cap in the bakery department displayed

Image © Тодорчук Екатерина/iStock

cellophane-encased Christmas cakes all sprinkled up for the children. Imagine Christmas-tree-shaped brownies! I knew if I had my two youngest granddaughters with me, those cakes would be in my cart quicker than I could say Tiny Tim.

When I got to the dairy aisle and spotted the eggnog, I swooned. A jot of rum and a dash of nutmeg with a pillow of whipped cream on top danced in my head. I briefly wondered if I could make it "seethe" like the ghost's punchbowl. It now comes in so many flavors too. If my husband would only consent to try the pumpkin, I'd have bought it. But I knew better. Among the holiday candy and greeting cards, I found a chocolate snowman

and let it ride in the top of my cart on its way to becoming a small gift for my hairdresser. Then, as I rounded the corner of the last aisle, I realized there would be great joy at the checkout as the cashier rang up at least ten items I hadn't really intended to buy. I was in the thrall of the bounty, after all.

It absolutely made my day to wander through this vast and varied harvest. It was humbling to contemplate all the time and effort that farmers, packers, truckers, cashiers, and store owners go through to produce this magnificent holiday display for us. And it's all because of the birth of one Boy. Amazing! I walked out feeling grateful, blessed, and more than a little bit hungry.

Family · Recipes

Apple Crisp

4 medium apples cored, pared, and thinly sliced

¾ cup old-fashioned or quick oats

¾ cup packed brown sugar

½ cup all-purpose flour

½ cup butter

Preheat oven to 350°F. Arrange apple slices in a greased 8-inch round cake pan. Combine oats, sugar, and flour. Cut in butter. Sprinkle mixture over apples. Bake 35 to 40 minutes until apples are tender and topping crisp. Serve warm with vanilla ice cream. Makes 6 servings.

Orange and Greek Yogurt Sea Salt Cake

½ cup orange juice, divided

½ cup plain Greek yogurt

3 large eggs

1 cup sugar

1½ cups all-purpose flour

2 teaspoons baking powder

2 teaspoons orange zest

⅓ cup vegetable oil

1 teaspoon sea salt, medium grain

¾ cup confectioners' sugar

Fresh orange segments for garnish

Preheat oven to 350°F. Butter a 9-inch round cake pan; line bottom with parchment paper. Set aside. In a large bowl, combine ¼ cup orange juice, yogurt, eggs, and sugar; mix well. Add flour, baking powder, and orange zest; stir to combine. Stir in oil; mix well. Pour batter into pan; lightly sprinkle sea salt over top. Bake 30 to 35 minutes, or until toothpick inserted into center comes out clean. Cool in pan 8 minutes. Turn cake out onto wire rack and cool completely; place on serving plate. Combine ¼ cup orange juice and confectioners' sugar, mixing until smooth. Drizzle glaze over top of cake. Garnish with orange segments. Makes 8 servings.

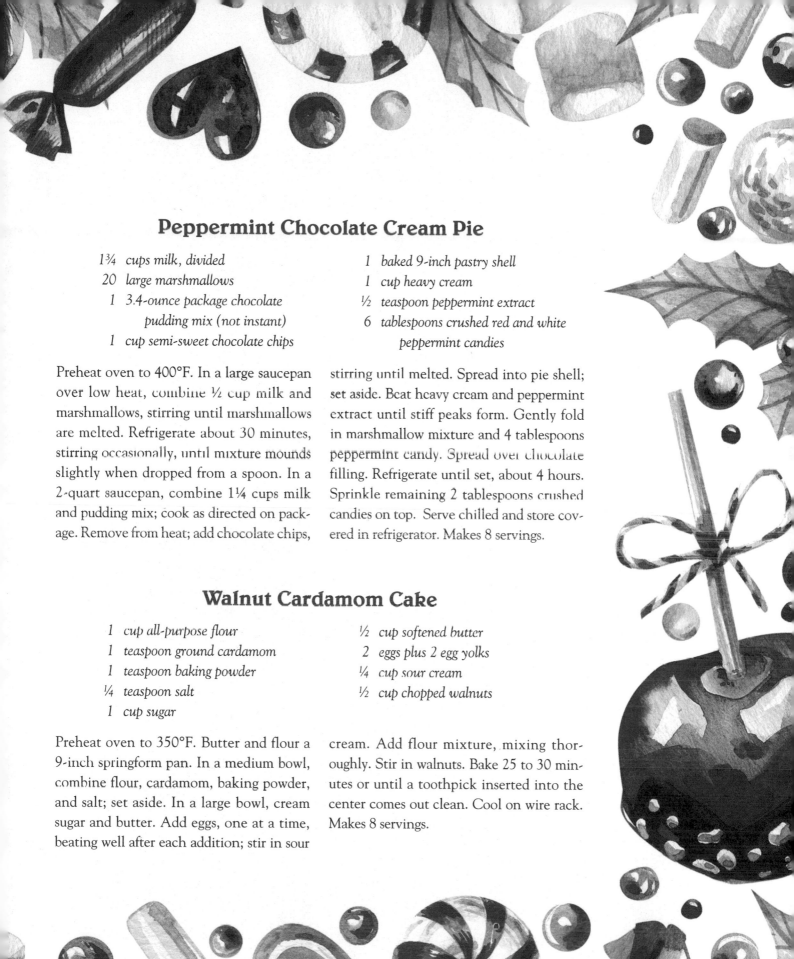

Peppermint Chocolate Cream Pie

1¾ cups milk, divided
20 large marshmallows
1 3.4-ounce package chocolate
   pudding mix (not instant)
1 cup semi-sweet chocolate chips

1 baked 9-inch pastry shell
1 cup heavy cream
½ teaspoon peppermint extract
6 tablespoons crushed red and white
   peppermint candies

Preheat oven to 400°F. In a large saucepan over low heat, combine ½ cup milk and marshmallows, stirring until marshmallows are melted. Refrigerate about 30 minutes, stirring occasionally, until mixture mounds slightly when dropped from a spoon. In a 2-quart saucepan, combine 1¼ cups milk and pudding mix; cook as directed on package. Remove from heat; add chocolate chips, stirring until melted. Spread into pie shell; set aside. Beat heavy cream and peppermint extract until stiff peaks form. Gently fold in marshmallow mixture and 4 tablespoons peppermint candy. Spread over chocolate filling. Refrigerate until set, about 4 hours. Sprinkle remaining 2 tablespoons crushed candies on top. Serve chilled and store covered in refrigerator. Makes 8 servings.

Walnut Cardamom Cake

1 cup all-purpose flour
1 teaspoon ground cardamom
1 teaspoon baking powder
¼ teaspoon salt
1 cup sugar

½ cup softened butter
2 eggs plus 2 egg yolks
¼ cup sour cream
½ cup chopped walnuts

Preheat oven to 350°F. Butter and flour a 9-inch springform pan. In a medium bowl, combine flour, cardamom, baking powder, and salt; set aside. In a large bowl, cream sugar and butter. Add eggs, one at a time, beating well after each addition; stir in sour cream. Add flour mixture, mixing thoroughly. Stir in walnuts. Bake 25 to 30 minutes or until a toothpick inserted into the center comes out clean. Cool on wire rack. Makes 8 servings.

Christmas Gifts

Evelyn V. Mackewicz

Amid the hurry and all the scurry
that Christmas somehow brings,
I couldn't help but wonder
about so many things.

I thought about the other gifts,
the kind you cannot buy,
of warmth and love and family
and friends we value high.

Those gifts unwrapped—with love's impact—
such things as joy and laughter,
no purchase price, yet twice as nice,
within the heart forever after.

Along about Christmas

Lillie D. Chaffin

Along about Christmas, you'll hear it said,
small children must always go early to bed.
Strange things are happening which fill them with joy,
but they must not be watching, not one girl or boy.

Along about Christmas, the crispy air
is chock-full of secrets; everywhere
it's "Don't open the closet," "I'll get your things,"
you're asked to tell wishes. Time seems to have wings!

Along about Christmas, there's laughter and cheer
that keep it the happiest time of the year!

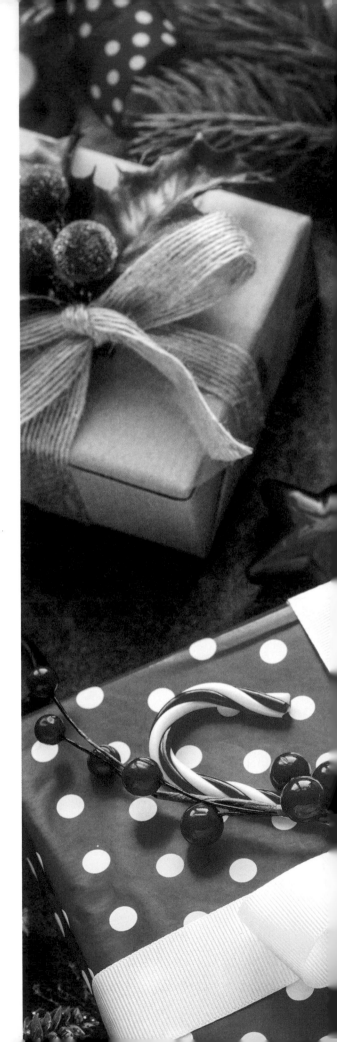

Image © kuvona/Adobe Stock

A Magical Christmas Moment
Elaine Marie Larson

When the mall traffic's been fought,
the Christmas colds caught,
the children are good
the Christmas tree stood . . .

when the last present's bought,
Christmas pageant lines taught,
the house-cleaning's done,
the garlands now hung . . .

when the Christmas lights light,
the gifts are wrapped tight,
the cookies are tasted,
the turkey is basted . . .

Then, for one precious,
magical moment,
I am settled.

Christmas
Marchette Gaylord Chute

My goodness, my goodness,
it's Christmas again.
The bells are all ringing.
I do not know when
I've been so excited.
The tree is all fixed,
the candles are lighted,
the pudding is mixed.

The wreath's on the door
and the carols are sung;
the presents are wrapped
and the holly is hung.
The turkey is sitting
all safe in its pan,
and I am behaving
as calm as I can.

Image © Dan Duchars/GAP Interiors
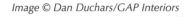

Jolly Old Saint Nicholas

Author Unknown

Jolly old Saint Nicholas, lean your ear this way!
Don't you tell a single soul what I'm going to say.
Christmas Eve is coming soon; now, you dear old man,
whisper what you'll bring to me, tell me if you can.

When the clock is striking twelve when I'm fast asleep,
down the chimney, broad and black, with your pack you'll creep;
all the stockings you will find hanging in a row,
mine will be the shortest one, you'll be sure to know.

Suzy wants a pair of skates; Johnny wants a sled.
Nellie wants a storybook, one she hasn't read.
As for me, I hardly know, so I think I'll rest;
choose for me, dear Santa Claus, what you think is best.

Jolly old Saint Nicholas, lean your ear this way!
Don't you tell a single soul what I'm going to say.
Christmas Eve is coming soon; now, you dear old man,
whisper what you'll bring to me, tell me if you can.

Image © Daniel Rodgers/Advocate Art

from
The True Saint Nicholas

William J. Bennett

When most of us hear the name "Saint Nicholas," we immediately think of Santa Claus. As children, we listened wide-eyed to Clement Clark Moore's famous poem about the night before Christmas, when "down the chimney St. Nicholas came with a bound." At some point along the way, we may have asked an older and wiser acquaintance why Santa sometimes goes by this alias. The answer we received was probably not very informative. And once we are all grown up, with children of our own, and by chance are asked the same question, we still are not sure. If pressed, we might guess that there was once a very good man named Nicholas, and his name somehow came to be connected with Santa Claus. But Saint Nicholas remains an elusive figure to us.

He is elusive even to scholars who study such matters. They believe that Saint Nicholas served as a bishop during the fourth century in the town of Myra, on the coast of the eastern Mediterranean Sea. He may have attended the famous Council of Nicaea convened by Constantine the Great in 325 to resolve issues troubling the Christian Church. But the details of his life and work remain sketchy. If he wrote anything it is long gone. The first known Nicholas "biography" dates to the eighth or ninth century, long after his death, when a Greek monk known as Michael the Archimandrite assembled a collection of tales about him.

We are left to piece together his life as best we can, using what we know and a good bit of surmise to arrive at the most likely story. Often we must rely on tradition as well as clues provided by the history of the times in which he lived. If the reputation he left behind means anything, we know there was something remarkable about this holy man. For hundreds of years, his name has been invoked, his deeds recounted. His shadow falls across epochs. . . .

Twilight falls on a remote village somewhere in northern France, about seven or eight centuries ago. It is December 5, the eve of Saint Nicholas Day. Anticipation is mounting, especially among the children. Moments ago, the little town center was crowded with spectators who gathered to watch the day's hero battle villains and demons in a play staged on the church steps. The play is done, and the villagers drift away, the youngsters tugging their parents' hands to hurry them along.

As soon as they get home, the children place their shoes carefully beside their bed or the fireplace. Then they dive under the covers, visions of treats dancing in their heads. Every boy and girl knows that later that night, when all are asleep, Saint Nicholas will pass through town.

When they wake the next morning, if they've been good, they'll find their shoes filled with all sorts of delights: fruit, nuts, sugar candy, maybe a coin or two. Those who've been unruly or failed to learn their catechism might find a small stick among the goodies, a miniature switch representing a rebuke for naughtiness.

Later that day, mothers will hand out cakes to eat beside the blazing hearth. The village boys will troop from door to door, singing in return for sweets. Neighbors will visit to exchange good cheer. Everyone will gather at church for hymns and prayers in remembrance of the beloved saint.

In this scene from the late Middle Ages, we find Saint Nicholas at work in the role we associate with him today. That role as a bringer of gifts doubtless grew out of the old stories about him, especially the story of his night visits to the home with three maidens where he left three bags of gold. Across Europe, people associated his name with generosity. The theologian Thomas Aquinas, in his thirteenth-century *Summa Theologica*, extolled Nicholas's gift-giving as an example of kindness made all the greater because it was offered in secret. The poet Dante, in his fourteenth-century *Purgatorio*, evoked "the liberality of Nicholas to the maidens" as a model of giving.

As time passed, stories of Nicholas the gift giver spread. German lore, for example, says that when St. Klaus (Nicholas) became a priest, family members in the wool trade presented him with a fine red woolen cape. Sometime later, a period of famine struck Lycia, and many poor people suffered from scurvy for lack of fruit. Nicholas had his red cape and other woolen material cut into pieces to make stockings. He filled the stockings with dried fruit treats and delivered them to needy children to help stem the scurvy. For families who had no firewood, he left charcoal, bundled with string, at the threshold. . . .

By the end of the sixteenth century, Nicholas had been banished from religious life in much of Western Europe. But he could not be driven out of people's hearts and imaginations. He was much too beloved for that to happen. When Saint Nicholas lost his honored place in churches, something extraordinary happened. He moved into homes, where he had legions of fans, especially among children. He became a hero of the hearth.

Altarpiece of St Nicolas in Monaco Cathedral.
Image © jorisvo/Adobe Stock

My Christmas Wish

Alice MacCulloch

What do I want most for Christmas?
What does my heart hold most dear?
These are the things I am wishing,
as each day of December draws near.

That I shall bring joy to the children,
that a smile may beam on each face;
and on the bright Christmas morning
each child in the world has a place.

Let me give my hand to the aged,
faces aglow with the spirit of youth;
warm hearts and the wealth of
    a handshake
and, O Lord, let me find truth.

Let snow fall, silent from heaven,
covering the earth with a fleece;
these are the gifts I want most
on this day, when the earth
    will know peace.

These are the gifts that are lasting
the whole of the long winter through,
when of yourself you are giving,
then life will give back to you.

CHRISTMAS GREETINGS by Corbert Gauthier.
Image © Corbert Gauthier. Courtesy of MHS Licensing.

Noel:
Christmas Eve, 1913
Robert Bridges

A frosty Christmas Eve
when the stars were shining,
fared I forth alone
where westward falls the hill,
and from many a village
in the water'd valley
distant music reached me,
peals of bells a-ringing;
the constellated sounds
ran sprinkling on earth's floor
as the dark vault above
with stars was spangled o'er.

Then sped my thought to keep
that first Christmas of all
when the shepherds watching
by their folds ere the dawn,
heard music in the fields,
and marveling could not tell
whether it were angels
or the bright stars singing.

But to me heard afar
it was starry music,
angels' song, comforting
as the comfort of Christ
when He spake tenderly
to his sorrowful flock;
the old words came to me
by the riches of time,
mellowed and transfigured,
as I stood on the hill
hearkening in the aspect
of the eternal silence.

Image © A2LE/Adobe Stock

The Lesser Christmas Miracle

Julie McDonald

It's easy for an Iowa child to believe what my Danish grandmother told me—that the farm animals celebrate the birth of Christ with human utterance at midnight on Christmas Eve. I first believed it on a farm near Fiscus, Iowa, and it flowed like a sweet undercurrent beneath the many preparations for the holidays.

A piece had to be learned for the Christmas program at Merrill's Grove Baptist Church, and I was admonished not to twist the hem of my skirt to immodest heights while delivering it. I performed without a lapse of memory and left my hemline alone; and when the program was over, we all got brown paper bags filled with hard candy. The bumpy raspberries with soft centers were my favorites, but I also admired the small rounds with a flower that remained visible until the candy was sucked to a sliver.

I had plans to visit the barn at midnight to hear what the cattle had to say to each other; but I kept them to myself, sensing that I would be thwarted should anyone find out. The paradoxically soft and stark light of the kerosene lamps shone on the clock face that I could not yet read, and I asked again and again, "Is it midnight yet?" I had never experienced a midnight, and that prospect, plus talking animals, was almost too much excitement to bear.

My parents spoke of Santa Claus, which presented a problem. If I went to the barn at midnight to listen to the animals, Santa Claus would have to wait to bring my presents, and he might not be able to work me into his route. What to do?

Exhaustion solved my dilemma. I awoke in my own bed in the cold light of Christmas morning and hurried to the dining room to see what Santa had brought with no more than a fleeting regret about missing the animal conversation. There would be other years, other midnights.

Later in the morning, I went to the barn, hoping that the cattle still might have the power to speak, but they did not. I had missed the moment, and now they only chewed and exhaled their grain-sweet breath in my face. "I'll come next year," I said, but I never did. The next year we moved to town.

In Harlan, Christmas meant colored lights strung from the Shelby County courthouse like a brilliant spider web, blue electric candles in Aunt Mary's window, and in Grandma's house, a Christmas tree with wax candles. We walked the streets of the town and admired the electric lights in other peoples' windows. In town, I could not go to the barn to listen to the animals talking, but I thought of them and wondered what they would say.

Many years later when I had children of my own, we were house-sitting for my in-laws in Davenport at Christmas, and I was the last one up, filling stockings. As midnight struck with Westminster chimes, I considered going to the stable. I even reached for my coat, but hung it up again. Mute horses would have stolen something precious from me. This dearest Christmas fancy of an Iowa child was something I wanted to keep, and I have. Surely the miraculous reason for Christmas can support this endearing lesser miracle.

Image © Dierdre Malfatto/Stocksy

Hymn for the Nativity

Edward Thring

Happy night and happy silence downward
softly stealing, softly stealing over land and sea;
stars from golden censers swing a silent eager
feeling down on Judah, down on Galilee;
and all the wistful air and earth and sky
listened, listened for the gladness of a cry.

Holy night, a sudden flash of light its way is
winging; angels, angels, all above, around;
hark, the angel voices, hark, the angel voices
singing, and the sheep are lying on the ground.
Lo, all the wistful air and earth and sky,
listen, listen to the gladness of the cry.

Wide, as if the light were music, flashes adoration
"Glory be to God, nor ever cease."
All the silence thrill, and speeds the message of
salvation: "Peace on earth, good will to men of peace."
Lo, all the wistful air and earth and sky,
listen, listen to the gladness of the cry.

Holy night, thy solemn silence evermore enfoldeth
angels' songs and peace from God on high:
holy night, thy watcher still with faithful eye
beholdeth wings that wave, and angel glory nigh,
lo, hushed is strife in air and earth and sky,
still thy watchers hear the gladness of the cry.

Praise Him, ye who watch the night,
the silent night of ages,
praise Him, shepherds, praise the Holy Child,
praise Him, ye who hear the light,
O praise Him, all ye sages; praise Him, children,
praise Him meek and mild.
Lo, peace on earth, glory to God on high;
listen, listen to the gladness of the cry.

Nativity Scene. Stained glass window in the Cathedral. Basel, Switzerland.
Image © MikeDot/iStock.

In the beginning was the Word, and the Word was with God, and the Word was God. He was in the beginning with God. All things were made through him, and without him was not any thing made that was made.

JOHN 1:1–3

So all the generations from Abraham to David were fourteen generations, and from David to the deportation to Babylon fourteen generations, and from the deportation to Babylon to the Christ fourteen generations.

Now the birth of Jesus Christ took place in this way. When his mother Mary had been betrothed to Joseph, before they came together she was found to be with child from the Holy Spirit. And her husband Joseph, being a just man and unwilling to put her to shame, resolved to divorce her quietly. But as he considered these things, behold, an angel of the Lord appeared to him in a dream, saying, "Joseph, son of David, do not fear to take Mary as your wife, for that which is conceived in her is from the Holy Spirit. She will bear a son, and you shall call his name Jesus, for he will save his people from their sins." All this took place to fulfill what the Lord had spoken by the prophet: "Behold, the virgin shall conceive and bear a son, and they shall call his name Immanuel" (which means, God with us). When Joseph woke from sleep, he did as the angel of the Lord commanded him: he took his wife, but knew her not until she had given birth to a son. And he called his name Jesus.

—MATTHEW 1:17–25

Image © Daniel Rodgers/Advocate Art

And the Word became flesh and dwelt among us, and we have seen his glory, glory as of the only Son from the Father, full of grace and truth.

JOHN 1:14

And in the same region there were shepherds out in the field, keeping watch over their flock by night. And an angel of the Lord appeared to them, and the glory of the Lord shone around them, and they were filled with great fear. And the angel said to them, "Fear not, for behold, I bring you good news of great joy that will be for all the people. For unto you is born this day in the city of David a Savior, who is Christ the Lord. And this will be a sign for you: you will find a baby wrapped in swaddling cloths and lying in a manger." And suddenly there was with the angel a multitude of the heavenly host praising God and saying, "Glory to God in the highest, and on earth peace among those with whom he is pleased!"

When the angels went away from them into heaven, the shepherds said to one another, "'Let us go over to Bethlehem and see this thing that has happened, which the Lord has made known to us." And they went with haste and found Mary and Joseph, and the baby lying in a manger. And when they saw it, they made known the saying that had been told them concerning this child. And all who heard it wondered at what the shepherds told them. But Mary treasured up all these things, pondering them in her heart. And the shepherds returned, glorifying and praising God for all they had heard and seen, as it had been told them.

—LUKE 2:8–20

Image © Daniel Rodgers/Advocate Art

> ### The next day he [John] saw Jesus coming toward him, and said, "Behold, the Lamb of God, who takes away the sin of the world!"
> JOHN 1:29

Now after Jesus was born in Bethlehem of Judea in the days of Herod the king, behold, wise men from the east came to Jerusalem, saying, "Where is he who has been born king of the Jews? For we saw his star when it rose and have come to worship him." When Herod the king heard this, he was troubled, and all Jerusalem with him; and assembling all the chief priests and scribes of the people, he inquired of them where the Christ was to be born. They told him, "In Bethlehem of Judea, for so it is written by the prophet: 'And you, O Bethlehem, in the land of Judah, are by no means least among the rulers of Judah; for from you shall come a ruler who will shepherd my people Israel.'"

Then Herod summoned the wise men secretly and ascertained from them what time the star had appeared. And he sent them to Bethlehem, saying, "Go and search diligently for the child, and when you have found him, bring me word, that I too may come and worship him." After listening to the king, they went on their way. And behold, the star that they had seen when it rose went before them until it came to rest over the place where the child was. When they saw the star, they rejoiced exceedingly with great joy. And going into the house, they saw the child with Mary his mother, and they fell down and worshiped him. Then, opening their treasures, they offered him gifts, gold and frankincense and myrrh. And being warned in a dream not to return to Herod, they departed to their own country by another way.

—MATTHEW 2:1–12

Image © Daniel Rodgers/Advocate Art

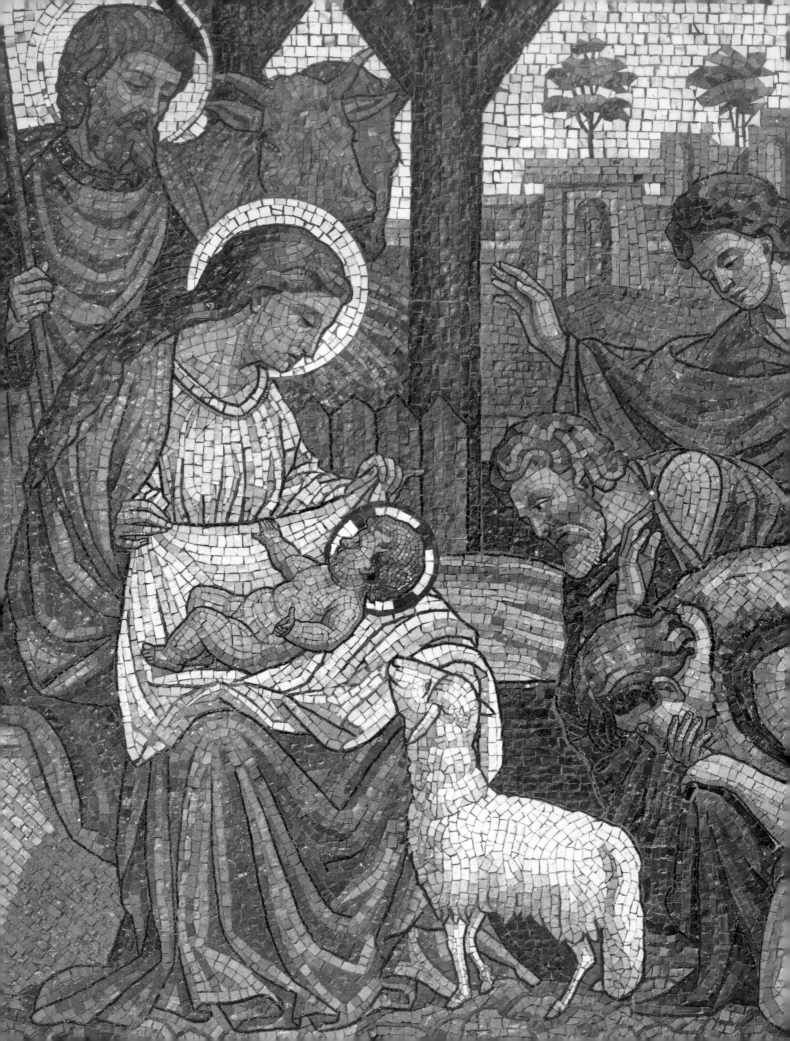

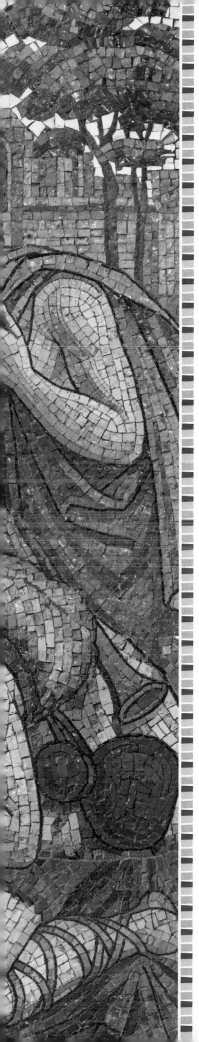

Paradox
Angelus Silesius

Here lies the precious Babe, first-fruit of virgin's womb,
angels' delight and joy, men's highest price and boon,
should He your Savior be and lift you into God,
O man, stay near the crib and make it your abode.

How simple we must grow! How simple they, who came!
The shepherds looked at God long before any man.
He sees God nevermore not there, nor here on earth
who does not long within to be a shepherd first.

All things are now reversed: the castle's in the cave,
the crib becomes the throne, the night brings forth the day,
the virgin bears a child; O man! reflect and say
that heart and mind must be reversed in every way.

One Small Child
Esther S. Buckwalter

One little child, no more, no less—
and could His mother Mary guess
salvation for the human race
depended on that night, that place?
And did she know
    this child would cause
all heaven to rock
    with glad applause?
Would cause the angels to rehearse
their midnight song of sacred verse?
Would cause a star of strange design
to leave its orbit and to shine
a brilliant path, from east to west?
Would cause wise men
    to choose the best
of hoarded treasure, and to search
the nations from a camel perch?
Would make a king
    (in craven fear)
destroy small man-children near?
To this small child
    the nation thrilled,
for He was prophecy fulfilled.

But could His mother even guess,
while rocking Him
    with tenderness,
the whole import of His advent,
this one small child from
    heaven sent.

Image © Adobe Stock

Through My Window

No Strangers at the Manger

Pamela Kennedy

By the time you're my age, you've seen dozens of Christmas pageants, heard scores of Christmas sermons, memorized a repertoire of carols, and read the Christmas story enough times to know it by heart: There was a father and mother with no place to stay; there were shepherds and angels, a star, a manger, a baby, and eventually some wise men showed up. The little Lord Jesus, no crying He makes. Christmas is predictable. But then, unexpectedly, a little child shows you something new about that old, old story.

This past Christmas, when I set up the nativity scene that has been in the family for over fifty years, I placed it on a small vintage drop-leaf table that happened to be at eye-level for our three-year-old granddaughter, Helen. She had heard the Christmas story and even had her own toy wooden manger scene at home. But this one was different. These old-fashioned figures were not large and child safe. They were small, detailed, and life-like. The animals boasted realistic features and the people were sculpted with a variety of facial characteristics and dressed in brightly colored Medieval-style garments. A tiny baby Jesus rested in a little brown manger. She was captivated.

Each day I found the characters rearranged. Sometimes a sheep was in the manger and baby Jesus was riding the cow. One day a wise man stood in for Joseph while Mother Mary took a nap under some straw. And then different figures started to show up. A snowman and a ballerina joined the Holy Family around the tiny crib. A model of the space shuttle landed on the manger roof. The drop leaf was raised and half a dozen toy cars pulled up as if attending a drive-in movie. Another day I heard, "Ho, ho, ho! Santa's here. Have you been good? Ho, ho, ho!" I peeked around the corner to find Helen introducing the Holy Family to jolly old St. Nick. At one point, baby Jesus went missing. But Helen, undaunted by misplacing the Savior of the world, retrieved a tiny plastic baby from the toy box and placed him in the manger. "His name is Eric," she told us. Something was always happening around the manger and, apparently, everyone was welcomed there.

I find it easy to become so consumed with holiday routines that the wonder gets lost among the decorating, shopping, gift wrapping, and menu planning. There are so many expectations to be met and the feeling that I'm somehow responsible for everyone having a good time overwhelms me. Will the gifts be well received? Will it snow? How will we seat the whole family around our small table? Can we juggle cooking times for every-

Image © Scott Turner/iStock

thing with just one oven? Will the roast be done on time? My joy begins to dissipate as my busyness increases.

And then my attention is captured by a little girl wearing pajamas and fairy wings who just assumes that everyone should be delighted to be celebrating the holiday. With fresh eyes she sees new possibilities. Christmas is open to all comers. There's no need to dress up or down, to please everyone, or meet unrealistic expectations. Time is fluid. Who needs a schedule? Why wouldn't Mary and Joseph be happy to meet a snowman in Bethlehem or entertain a jolly gift-giver with flying reindeer? Because when Jesus comes to visit, He brings joy to the world! Heaven and nature sing, and everything is somehow set right. There is always enough love to go around. And there are no strangers at the manger.

Else Why Should I Dare Now to Kneel?

Rosemary Clifford Trott

God, I do not ask it more
that I should find upon the floor
beneath the tree my heart's desire;
nor that, within the Christmas fire,
my fondest dreams should all come true.
I do not ask these things of You.

I only ask that, having known
earth's sweetest love, I can atone
for any lack that I have caused,
for any time I have not paused

to heal some pain,
or thought of my own selfish gain.

Else why should I dare now to kneel
before the Christ Child's créche and feel
the gentle warmness of His breath,
the sacredness of birth and death,
or wonder of the years between,
recalling all the stars, the snow,
the gifts of love, the songs, the glow.

Carols by Candlelight

Edna Jaques

Carols by candlelight—what lovelier thing
could the wide realm of earth or heaven bestow
than a dim church fragrant with evergreen
and Christmas carols sung by candle glow?

The choir loft is dim, and shadows fall
upon the pillars twined with fir and pine,
and every nook and corner of the church
holds little golden pools of candle shine.

The people listen as the music fills
the high domed ceiling and the quiet stalls

as melodies, as old as Christmastime,
echo within the fragrant sacred walls,

Glory to God! Peace, peace on earth, goodwill—
the words float upward in the silent night
while lonely hearts are lifted up once more
in the soft atmosphere of candlelight.

In the warm atmosphere of song and praise,
the lonely hearted and the tired sing
the age-old melodies of Christmastime,
of kings and shepherds and a newborn king.

SILENT NIGHT *by Abraham Hunter. Image copyright © Abraham Hunter/MHS Licensing*

Peace on Christmas Day

Marianne Coyne

There is peace in my heart on this Christmas Day,
as a star proclaims a birth.
There is peace in my heart on this Christmas Day,
filling my soul with mirth.

There's a song from my lips on this Christmas Day,
echoing hosts on high.
There's a song from my lips on this Christmas Day,
proclaiming God's mercy is nigh.

Sing along all creation, sing along while you can;
join a choir of angels wishing peace toward all men.
Come along and be merry; come along, let's draw near
to the spirit of the Christ Child dear.

There's no time to tarry on this Christmas Day,
so, open your arms and embrace
God's own perfect love on this Christmas Day,
come to save the whole human race.

In the form of a child, on this Christmas Day,
came a savior for every lost soul.
God rejoined us to Him, on this Christmas Day,
destroying each sin and its toll.

Sing along all creation, sing along while you can;
join a choir of angels wishing peace toward all men.
Come along and be merry; come along, let's draw near
to the spirit of the Christ Child dear.

Image © GAP Photos

Traditions that Bind

Anne Kennedy Brady

My father-in-law welcomes any opportunity to remind us of his British roots. Melvin moved to Seattle from London over fifty years ago; but he still maintains that cricket is better than baseball, the parliamentary system is a superior form of government, and (perhaps most importantly) Christmas isn't Christmas without plum pudding. For the uninitiated, plum pudding is a dense dome of dried fruits and nuts held together with sweet, rich cake. Each Christmas after dinner, Melvin douses the entire thing in brandy and sets it ablaze, as my mother-in-law, Cordelia, frets on the sidelines. Once the alcohol burns off and the flame dies down, he proudly serves a slice (or two) to anyone interested, along with a generous slurp of heavy cream. To hear him tell it, it's the only true English way to enjoy the dessert. Cordelia's mother, however, also a proud Brit, preferred to top her pudding with hard sauce—essentially a spiked buttercream frosting. Each year they'd debate whose way was the right way, and the argument became as much a tradition as the food itself.

It's been sixteen years since Grandma Helen passed away, and heavy cream on Christmas pudding has become the undisputed way of things. But this year, I decided to stir things up. Our daughter is named for this feisty, frosting-loving lady; why not honor her with a little Christmas drama? After checking with my husband and brother-in-law to make sure I wasn't poking too big of a hornet's nest, I found a recipe and planned a clandestine shopping trip.

Standing in line at the crowded grocery store, loaded down with butter, powdered sugar, and rum extract, I got to thinking about my own childhood traditions. I always held them close, bewitched by their uncanny power to bind our family together no matter where my dad's military career moved us. As my brothers and I grew up, those traditions shifted; but they never completely disappeared. As more people (and kids) joined the family, we moved stocking gifts to Christmas Eve, while saving the "tree presents" until morning. And in fact, Christmas Eve isn't even the 24th anymore—we meet up a week later, at my parents' beach house! These accommodations felt strange at first, but it didn't take long for everyone to embrace them. The schedule shift meant more time relaxing together and less overwhelmed kids (and parents). It meant my brothers and I could spend each Christmas season with both sides of our families. It meant honoring the things we love to do and the people we love to do them with.

On the drive home, I thought about other traditions we've learned to hold more loosely. Early in our relationship, my husband and I loved to hop in the car after Christmas Eve service and drive around looking at lights. But then we had two young children, who brought with them early bedtimes and an aversion to long, destination-less car rides. So now we check out the light show at the zoo early in December and then grab dinner at a nearby pizza place. We pepper modern Christmas carols our kids enjoy in amongst the classics we love. We've told stories of our own childhood Christmases at dinnertime. We found a Christmas movie we love to watch once the kids are in bed. We make cookies that remind us of home. We prioritize family time, whatever that looks like right now.

Image © freeskyline/Adobe Stock

And that year after dinner, when I revealed my latest culinary contribution to the Brady family Christmas, Melvin gamely stepped up to defend his heavy-cream-only position as he had years ago. Cordelia, my mother-in-law, seemed delighted to enjoy her mother's favorite dessert again. The teenage nephews each diplomatically chose a side, my six-year-old nervously tried both and enjoyed neither, and three-year-old Helen, named for the instigator herself, opted for a cookie instead. Later that evening, I asked my husband if he thought I should make hard sauce again next year. He smiled. "Definitely," he nodded, his eyes misting a bit. "It was like Grandma was here again."

I used to see traditions as ties that bind us together, but that metaphor no longer fits quite right. Instead, I think I'll look at them as springs on a trampoline—able to bend and stretch as we bounce around this life, bringing us joy, and providing us a safe place to land. As our family grows and changes, beloved traditions lift us up, rather than bind us in, which is good, because after two helpings of pudding and hard sauce, I don't want anything binding me in for a while.

We Love Christmas
Lela Bernard

We love Christmas
with brown roast turkey resting in
a nest of dressing deep,
and bowls of mashed potatoes piled
high in a buttered heap.
Rich pumpkin pies and spicy cakes—
the table almost groans;
but when we're all
    through eating,
there is nothing left
    but bones.

Christmas Dinner
Alice Kennelly Roberts

The heart remembers Christmas
and days of long ago,
when festive preparations
made all the house aglow;
the kitchen fairly bubbled
with turkey, puddings, pies,
and all those extra goodies
which came as a surprise.

Each person had his duties,
and young and old could share;
the little ones and Grandma
and even Spot were there;
the fruitcake and
    the mincemeat,

the chestnut dressing, too,
the pumpkins and red apples
filled childhood's world anew.

Yes, hearts go home
    at Christmas
to take again their place,
to see at Christmas dinner
each dear, remembered face;
and though the scene
    we cherish
a short while will be there,
the words, the joy, the laughter
are with us everywhere.

Image © Friedrich Strauss/GAP Photos

The Spirit of Giving

Anne Kennedy Brady

Since moving to Chicago a decade ago, one of my favorite Christmas traditions has been shopping on "The Magnificent Mile." My husband and I set aside one Saturday in December to head downtown and marvel at the opulent decorations festooning the specialty boutiques and department stores. In the early years, after browsing and buying a few gifts for each other, we splurged on lunch at a local steakhouse. When kids came along, we bundled them up and adjusted the schedule to accommodate naptimes and picky eaters.

In the past, we'd separate, each bringing a kid to "help" as we shopped for the other parent. With Helen in tow, I'd pick out a book or a cozy sweatshirt I knew Kevin would like. Kevin would take Milo to the costume jewelry section of the closest department store and let him choose anything under $20. Milo loves gems, so these gifts have ranged from a pair of gigantic sparkling pink earrings roughly two inches in diameter, to an evening purse featuring a smiley face made entirely of rhinestones.

But last year, after reading an article about the importance of instilling in children a sense of generosity, we decided to have the kids shop for each other. Milo is six and Helen is three and, somehow, these felt like appropriate ages to embrace the superior joy of gift-giving over receiving. What terrific memories we would build! What wonderful parents we would be!

I paired up with Milo this time, and we headed to the toy store. Milo is a sweet kid. He is also firmly six years old. Despite the old adage claiming it is more blessed to give than to receive, he much prefers things the other way around. So I tried to prepare him for what I knew might be a challenging experience. We agreed that we were shopping not for him, but for his sister. We discussed what Helen likes (princesses) and decided what he would like to get for her (a princess doll). But as soon as we reached the store entrance, I saw his eyes widen at the sight of so many new toys. I crouched down to position myself three inches from Milo's face. "Princess doll," I said like an incantation. He nodded tremulously, and in we went.

I don't know if you have shopped in an upscale toy shop recently, but it's a far cry from the neon pink and blue warehouses of my own youth. Packaging tends toward neutral, muted colors and the organization strategy is inscrutable. It was impossible to beeline toward anything specific. In the fifteen minutes it took me to discern that there were zero princess dolls in stock, Milo had fallen deeply in love with a robotic tarantula, a book of spy-themed crafts, one enormous red dragon, and something called an "infinity cube." I finally managed to drag him to the densest concentration of pastel-hued toys and proceeded to dangle various options in front of his face. "How about this pretend makeup kit?" I asked cheerfully, only to be met with a frown. "Or a tea set? Here's a magic wand!" At last, he glumly grabbed something off the shelf and shoved it into my hands. Easily the tackiest thing in the store, a gaudy lavender unicorn gazed at me from its fuchsia packaging. "It walks," he mumbled.

"Helen will like it." Since his only other suggestion was a remote-control scorpion, we bought the unicorn and left the store.

Our departure, however, only seemed to deepen his sorrow. He had spotted a set of transforming robots while waiting in line, and as we walked to the escalators he pleaded for a shred of hope: "Can you just say maybe? PLEASE SAY MAYBE!" And with that, he fell to his knees and let the tragedy of Christmas giving overtake him. We spent the next half hour sitting together on the tiled shopping mall floor, his head in my lap. Across from us, a handful of animated elves advertised a new holiday movie while carols jing-jingled from the loudspeakers above. Eventually Milo's cries slowed to whimpers and we trudged outside to meet Kevin and Helen at the car.

A week later, I was wrapping presents while Helen napped, and Milo wandered in. "That's the one I picked out," he said, pointing to the unicorn. I glanced at him as one might regard a wild animal. "Do ... do you want to wrap it?" I asked. His eyes lit up. He snatched the paper and tape and got to work. On Christmas morning, he proudly presented the crinkly package to his sister and excitedly helped her rip off the paper. Helen, with her typical flair for the dramatic, gasped and shouted, "This is what I wanted my whole life!"

Over the next few hours, the unicorn whinnied and shuffled around the living room, confidently strolling off bookshelves and tables to the delighted squeals of both brother and sister.

Just before bed, after baths and the brushing of teeth, Helen hug-tackled her big brother and declared, "I wuv my unicorn!" He squeezed her tight in return. "I knew you would!" he replied with a self-satisfied grin. I couldn't help chuckling. Perhaps the path to becoming a joyful giver won't be as smooth as I anticipated; but in the meantime, these baby steps toward generosity will do just fine. Still, next year we might just stick to costume jewelry.

Image © Ruth Black/Stocksy

Christmas Night
Georgia B. Adams

It's snowing without, and the winds do howl;
how comfortable by the fire!
See how shadows are cast on the walls
as the flames rise higher and higher.

We'll talk of our friends and our blessings, too,
and the beauties of true goodwill;
it's a great night for gathering round the fire
while the winds outside grow chill.

The Yule Log's Charm
Vera Hardman

The Yule log is glowing
with warmth and
 good cheer,
for it is that wonderful time
 of the year,
when families grow closer
in thought and in heart,
as peace and contentment
this season imparts.

While we watch the soft
snowflakes tumbling down,
bringing enchantment and
charm to our town,

we find our thoughts
wandering away in a dream
and see them reflected
in the flames' gleam.

Though north winds
 are blowing
so strong and so bold,
the warmth of the Yule log
keeps out the cold,
as winter enwraps our
whole world in white,
our hearts know the magic
this splendorous night.

Image © Hazel Lincoln/Advocate Art

God Bless Your Christmas
Hazel Adams

God bless your Christmas wherever you are
and keep your courage bright;
for the spirit of man is the candle of God,
and it burns in the darkest night.

God bless your Christmas
wherever you are
and keep you strong in faith;
for the Spirit of God is the
refuge of man
and the light is His
dwelling place.

ISBN-13: 978-1-5460-0356-4

Published by Ideals
Hachette Book Group
1290 Avenue of the Americas
New York, NY 10104

Copyright © 2023 by Hachette Book Group, Inc.
All rights reserved. No part of this publication may be reproduced or transmitted in any form or by any means, electronic or mechanical, including photocopy, recording, or any information storage and retrieval system, without permission in writing from the publisher.

Printed and bound in the U.S.A.

Publisher, Peggy Schaefer
Senior Editor, Melinda Rathjen
Editor, Patricia A. Pingry
Designer and Photo Research, Marisa Jackson
Associate Editors & Permissions, Kristi Breeden and Eliza McLaughlin
Copy Editors, Amanda Varian

Cover: Image © GAP Interiors/The CONTENTed Nest
Inside cover art © Peter McGowan/Advocate Art
Additional art credits: Art for "Bits & Pieces" by Emily van Wyk

Want more homey philosophy, poetry, inspiration, and art? Be sure to look for our annual issue of *Easter Ideals* at your favorite store.

Join a community of *Ideals* readers on Facebook at: www.facebook.com/IdealsMagazine
Readers are invited to submit original poetry and prose for possible use in future publications. Please send no more than four typed submissions to: Hachette Book Group, Attn: *Ideals* Submissions, 830 Crescent Centre Dr., Suite 450, Franklin, Tennessee 37067. Editors cannot guarantee your material will be used, but we will contact you if we do wish to publish.

ACKNOWLEDGMENTS

BENNETT, WILLIAM J. From *The True Saint Nicholas: Why He Matters to Christmas* by William J. Bennett. Copyright © 2009, 2018 by William J. Bennett. Reprinted with the permission of Howard Books, a division of Simon & Schuster, Inc. All rights reserved. ESTEB, ADLAI A. "Snowflakes" excerpted from *Firewood* © 1952 by Review and Herald Publishing Association. OUR THANKS to the following authors or their heirs for permission granted or for material submitted for publication: Georgia B. Adams, Maxine Bell, Lela Bernard, Christine Phillips Blagden, Anne Kennedy Brady, Esther S. Buckwalter, Lillie D. Chassin, Marchette Gaylord Chute, Marianne Coyne, Renee A. Gardner, Marguerite Gode, Linda C. Grazulis, Edgar A. Guest, Vera Hardman, Edna Jaques, Pamela Kennedy, Elaine Marie Larson, Alice MacCulloch, Evelyn V. Mackewicz, Julie McDonald, Alice Kennelly Roberts, Eileen Spinelli, Susan Sundwall, Louise Weibert Sutton, Rosemary Clifford Trott, and Valerie Worth.

Scripture quotations, unless otherwise indicated, are taken from the ESV® Bible (*The Holy Bible, English Standard Version®*), copyright © 2001 by Crossway, a publishing ministry of Good News Publishers. Used by permission. All rights reserved. Scripture verse marked NIV taken from *The Holy Bible, New International Version®*, NIV®. Copyright © 1973, 1978, 1984, 2011 by Biblica, Inc.™ Used by permission of Zondervan. All rights reserved worldwide.

Every effort has been made to establish ownership and use of each selection in this book. If contacted, the publisher will be pleased to rectify any inadvertent errors or omissions in subsequent editions.